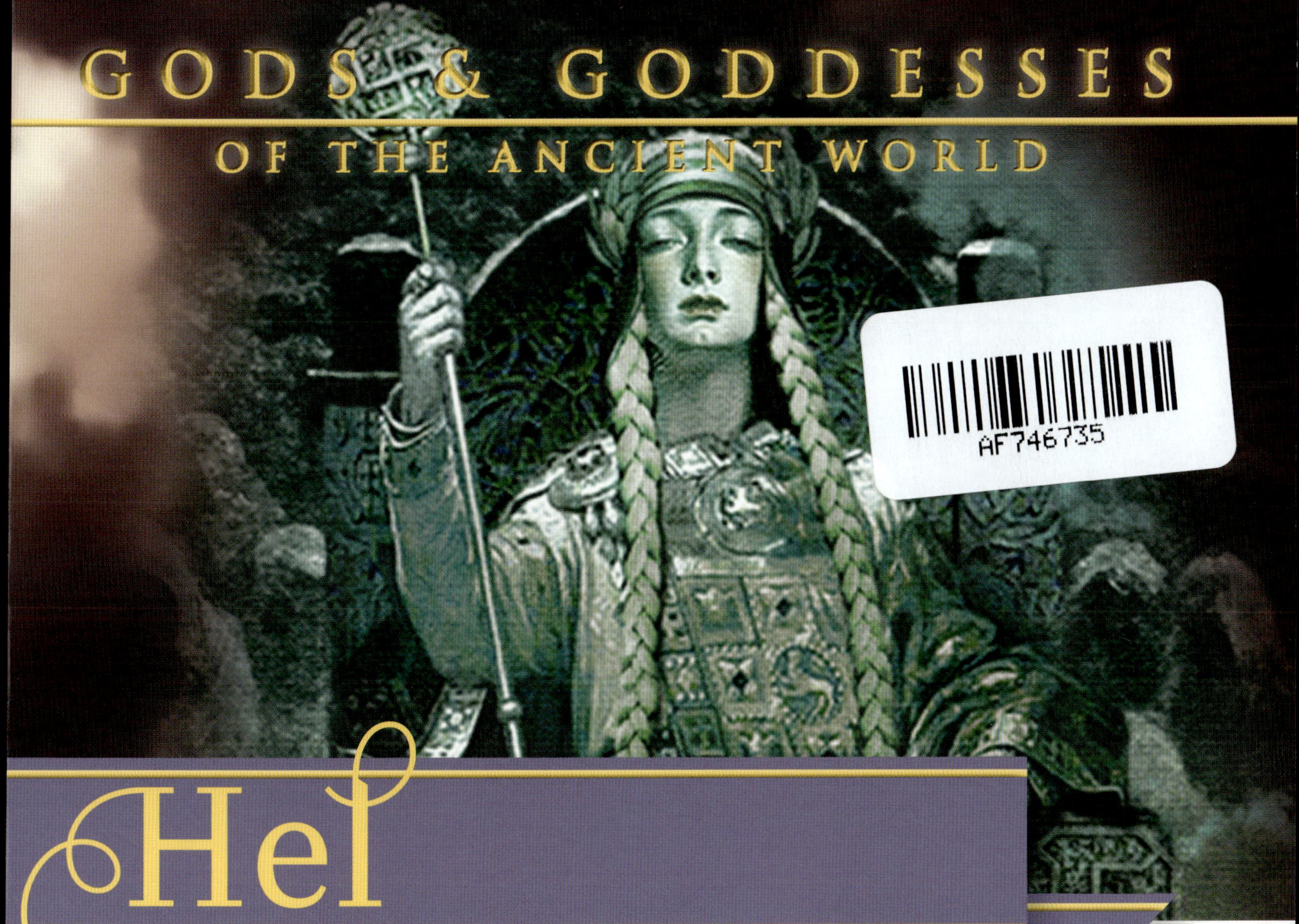

GODS & GODDESSES

OF THE ANCIENT WORLD

AF746735

Hel

BY VIRGINIA LOH-HAGAN

Gods and goddesses were the main characters of myths. Myths are traditional stories from ancient cultures. Storytellers answered questions about the world by creating exciting explanations. People thought myths were true. Myths explained the unexplainable. They helped people make sense of human behavior and nature. Today, we use science to explain the world. But people still love myths. Myths may not be literally true. But they have meaning. They tell us something about our history and culture.

45th Parallel Press

Published in the United States of America by Cherry Lake Publishing
Ann Arbor, Michigan
www.cherrylakepublishing.com

Content Adviser: Alexandra Krasowski, Worcester Art Museum, Harvard University (Extension School)
Reading Adviser: Marla Conn MS, Ed., Literacy specialist, Read-Ability, Inc.
Book Design: Jen Wahi

Photo Credits: © KYNA STUDIO/Shutterstock.com, 5; © eldar nurkovic/Shutterstock.com, 6; Arthur Rackham/Public Domain/Wikimedia Commons, 8; Carl Emil Doepler/Public Domain/Wikimedia Commons, 11, 19; © mangojuicy/Shutterstock.com, 13; © elebeZoom/Shutterstock.com, 15; © alexkich/Shutterstock.com, 17; © cervkuba/Shutterstock.com, 23; © Catmando/Shutterstock.com, 24; Emil Doepler/Public Domain/Wikimedia Commons, 27; Ludvig Abelin Schou/Public Domain/Wikimedia Commons, 29; © Howard David Johnson, 2018, Cover, 1, 21; Various art elements throughout, Shutterstock.com

Copyright © 2019 by Cherry Lake Publishing
All rights reserved. No part of this book may be reproduced or utilized in any form or by any means without written permission from the publisher.

45th Parallel Press is an imprint of Cherry Lake Publishing.

Library of Congress Cataloging-in-Publication Data has been filed and is available at catalog.loc.gov

Printed in the United States of America
Corporate Graphics

ABOUT THE AUTHOR:

Dr. Virginia Loh-Hagan is an author, university professor, former classroom teacher, and curriculum designer. She thinks she lives with hounds from hell. She lives in San Diego with her very tall husband and very naughty dogs. To learn more about her, visit www.virginialoh.com.

TABLE OF CONTENTS

CHAPTER 1

GODDESS OF THE DEAD

Who is Hel? What does she look like? Who are her family members?

Hel was a **Norse** goddess. Norse means coming from the Norway area. Hel was a goddess of the dead. She ruled the **underworld**. The underworld was a place where dead souls lived. It was where people went when they died. It was also called hell. Norse gods called it Helheim. This means "Hel's home." Helheim was cold. It was dark.

Hel ruled over people who died without glory. She ruled over people who died from sickness. She ruled over people who died from old age. She ruled over people who did crimes. Those who died in war were sent to a special underworld. They went to **Valhalla**. This means "hall of the dead." It was ruled by Odin. Odin was the father of all gods.

Hel's name means "hidden." The dead were hidden beneath the ground. They were hidden from the living. They were hidden from the world.

Hel was also a goddess of death.

Hel was also known as Hela.

Hel was a monster. Half her body was alive. That side was pretty. Half her body was dead. That side was ugly. Her bones were outside her body. Her skin was rotting. Hel smelled like a dead person. She wore black and white clothes.

She was not a happy person. She was grim. She was greedy. She was selfish. She was mean.

Both of Hel's parents were giants. Hel's father was Loki. Loki was a trickster god. He was also a giant. He played tricks.

Family Tree

Grandparents: Farbauti (frost giant; his name means "striker") and Laufey (frost giantess; her name means "leaves")

Parents: Loki (trickster god) and Angrboda (giantess; her name means "distress-bringer")

Brothers: Jormungand (world serpent) and Fenrir (wolf)

Half brothers: Sleipnir (Odin's eight-legged horse) and Narfi (his name means "corpse")

Nephews (sons of Fenrir): Skoll (sun-eater) and Hati (moon-eater)

Sometimes he was a friend of the gods. Sometimes he was an enemy of the gods.

Hel's mother was Angrboda. Angrboda was a **giantess**. Giantess means female giant. Loki and Angrboda had three scary children. Hel was the youngest child. Her brother was Fenrir. He was a giant wolf. He wouldn't stop growing. Her other brother was Jormungand. He was known as the world **serpent**. Serpents are snakes. Jormungand wrapped his body around the earth. He was in the world's oceans.

Hel came from a dangerous family.

CHAPTER 2

GATES OF HELL

What happens to Loki's children? What is the road to Helheim like? How does Hel collect dead souls?

Loki's children were born in a dark cave. They were born in the land of giants. Loki took them to **Asgard**. Asgard was the center of the universe. There were two tribes of Norse gods and goddesses. They were the Aesir and the Vanir. The Aesir lived in Asgard.

The gods were scared of Loki's children. They thought they were pain, sin, and death. They could see the future. They knew Loki's children would hurt the gods. They knew they'd bring doom. The gods kidnapped them. Then Odin kicked Loki's children out.

He sent Hel to Helheim. She lived with the dishonored dead. She shared her food with them. Odin chained Fenrir to a rock. Odin sent Jormungand to the sea.

Odin gave Hel power over the underworld. Hel treated kind people well. She treated bad people badly. She decided where to send each dead soul. The underworld had several sections. Hel had different places for different souls. She sent killers and thieves to bad places. She sent them to a

Odin banished Loki's children.

All in the Family

Fenrir was a giant wolf. He was the brother of Hel. His power was that he grew. He couldn't stop growing. He got bigger and bigger. The gods were scared of him. They tried to chain him. But he kept breaking chains. The gods had dwarfs make magical chains. They pretended to play a game. They asked Fenrir to chain himself. They told Fenrir to show off his power. Fenrir didn't trust them. He said he'd get in chains if a god stuck his hand in his mouth. Tyr was the god of justice. He did it. Fenrir agreed to play. The gods tricked him. They chained Fenrir. They bound him to a rock. Fenrir got mad. He ripped off Tyr's hand. The gods put a sword in his jaws. This kept his jaws open. His drool formed a river.

Dead souls wore "Hel-shoes." These were strong shoes.

shore of **corpses**. Corpses are dead bodies. She also sent them to a cave filled with snakes. Snake poison dripped down the walls.

The road to the underworld was rough. It was called Hellway. There was a river. It was the border between life and death. It was freezing cold. It had knives floating in it.

The only way to cross the river was over the bridge. The bridge was called Gjallarbru. It was made of crystal. It had a golden roof. It was hung on a single hair. It was the only bright thing in hell. Modgud guarded the bridge. She was all bones. Dead souls told her their names. They did this to cross.

Dead souls got to hell's gates. A scary dog guarded the gates. Dead souls entered the gates.

Sometimes Hel collected dead souls. She rode on her horse. Her horse was white. It had three legs. Hel used a rake. She raked up the dead. Sometimes she used a broom. She swept up the dead.

Dead souls walked in the cold and darkness.

CHAPTER 3

DAUGHTER OF EVIL

What happens to Baldur? How does Hel support Loki?

Baldur was the god of light. He was the son of Odin and Frigg. Frigg was the goddess of marriage. Baldur had dreams of dying. He told his parents. Odin was worried. He rode to hell. He wanted to raise a witch from the dead. He wanted to ask about Baldur's dreams. Odin saw a bloody dog running to him. He thought this was an **omen**. Omens are signs.

Frigg was also worried. She went around the world. She begged people not to hurt Baldur. But Frigg made a mistake. She didn't think mistletoe was a problem.

She thought it wasn't important. She thought it was too little to do harm.

She told Baldur he was safe. She hosted a party. Loki went to the party. He insulted the gods. He tricked Frigg. Frigg told him about mistletoe. Loki used that information. He made a mistletoe dart. He tricked Baldur's brother into throwing the dart. The dart killed Baldur.

The gods believed in the magic of seeing the future.

Real World Connection

Helsinki is the capital of Finland. A lot of people live in the city. The city has limited space. The city planners decided to build down. They built a city underground. It's called a shadow city. The shadow city has a swimming pool. It has a church. It has a hockey rink. It has a data center. It has a shopping area. It has parking caves. It has over 125 miles (201 kilometers) of tunnels. There are plans to make the whole city underground. This reduces the spreading of cities into farm areas. This uses the natural cooling of the city's rocks. City planners carve buildings into the earth. They use the rock under the city. They're protected from the sun and wind. They're also protected from attacks. The underground city could support 600,000 people. Finnish soldiers are training in the tunnels.

Baldur's brother was Hod. Hod was the god of night and winter.

Baldur's light was gone. This created winter. The winter lasted for 3 years. The gods were mad at Loki. Loki ran away. Loki was now an enemy of the gods. He was mad at the gods for kicking out his children. He wanted to get even.

The gods tried to get Baldur from hell. They sent Hermod. Hermod was the gods' messenger. He rode for 9 days. Modgud told him Baldur had crossed the bridge. Hermod passed hell's gates. He saw Baldur. Baldur was sitting next to Hel. He kneeled before Hel. He begged for Baldur's life. He said Baldur was loved and missed.

Hel wanted Hermod to prove it. She made a deal. She'd release Baldur if all living things cried for him. She knew this wouldn't happen. The gods begged everyone to cry for Baldur. But Loki stepped in. He disguised himself as a giantess. He didn't cry. So, Hel kept Baldur.

Hel owned the dead souls in Helheim.

CHAPTER 4

KEEPERS OF HELL

What is Eljudnir? Who is Garm? Who is Nidhogg?

Hel lived in a big castle. It was named Eljudnir. This means "damp with **sleet**." Sleet is frozen rain. The outside walls were icy. Hel's house had high walls. It had big gates. It had a big drop past the door. This meant people could fall to their death. Everything in her house had a name. Hel's bed was "sick." Her bed curtains were "glittering evil." Her window curtains were "bad luck." Her knife was "starvation." Her plate was "famine." Her table was "hunger."

Hel had two servants. Their names were Ganglati and Ganglot. Their names mean "lazy walker." They moved slowly. They looked like they were standing still.

Garm was a **hellhound**. Hellhounds were dogs of hell. Garm guarded hell's gates. He lived in a dark cave. He howled loudly. He was stained with blood. He could only be calmed by hel-cakes. These were special breads from hell. Garm fought with Tyr. Tyr was the god of justice. He tricked Fenrir. Garm and Tyr killed each other.

Norse gods live in halls. Halls are grand houses.

Garm means "rag."

Nidhogg was a dragon. He also lived in hell. He chewed at the roots of the World Tree. The World Tree held up all the Norse worlds. The roots trapped Nidhogg inside. Nidhogg chewed on the corpses in hell. He only chewed on the criminals. He carried their corpses under his wings. Hel was his master.

Cross-Cultural Connection

Mictecacihuatl was sacrificed as a baby. She became an Aztec goddess. Aztecs were ancient people from central Mexico. Mictecacihuatl means "lady of the dead." She ruled the land of the dead. She ruled with her husband. She guarded the bones of the dead. She collected bones. She gave them to other gods. The bones were returned to the land of the living. They were used to form new humans. But one time, the bones were dropped. They mixed together. Aztecs believe this is why we have different races.

People buried treasures with dead bodies. The treasures were gifts to Mictecacihuatl. Mictecacihuatl was only bones. She didn't have any skin or flesh. She wore a skirt made from snakes. Her jaws were wide open. She swallowed the stars. She made them invisible during the day. She ruled over the festivals of the dead. Today, these festivals are known as Day of the Dead.

CHAPTER 5

TO HELL AND BACK

What is Ragnarok? What does Hel do in the war?

Baldur's death broke the peace among gods and giants. Loki's trick started **Ragnarok**. This was the final battle. It was the end of the world. It was known as the "doom of the gods." Loki fought against the gods. He led an army of giants. Loki's children broke free from Odin's power. They helped Loki.

Loki was given a ship. The ship was called Naglfar. This means "nail mover." It was a big ship. It was made of dead people's nails. Hel cut dead people's toenails. She cut their fingernails. She saved all these nail clippings.

Hel opened hell's gates. This released all the dead souls. Hel gave Loki an army of dead soldiers. Loki sailed them in Naglfar. His army set the world on fire. The fire killed humans. It killed giants. It killed gods. The earth sank into the sea. Then it rose again. The world started over.

Loki and his children hated the gods for kicking them out.

Nobody knows what happened to Hel. There aren't any stories about her death. She was probably still in the

Explained By Science

Hel lived underground. She did this her whole life. Humans can't do that. Without sunlight, people would get sick. Human bodies would stop making vitamin D. They wouldn't get calcium. This could make them choke. Their bones could get weak. Their muscles could get weak. Children would have a harder time than adults. They could die from darkness. They could get rickets. Rickets deforms bones and teeth. It could lead to breathing problems. It could lead to heart problems. Sunlight triggers serotonin. Serotonin helps people sleep. It keeps people in a good mood. Without sunlight, people would sleep more. They'd feel lonelier. They'd feel more tired. They'd be sad. Without sunlight, there'd be no plants. Without plants, there'd be no food. People can't live without food. But too much sun is bad. This could cause sunburns. It could cause skin cancer.

Loki and his children killed the main gods.

underworld. She was probably waiting for dead souls. Ragnarok caused many deaths. And somebody had to greet them in the underworld.

Don't anger the goddesses. Hel had great powers. And she knew how to use them.

DID YOU KNOW?

- The word hell comes from Hel.
- Some people honored Hel. They did this at Samhain. Samhain was celebrated in Ireland and Scotland. It took place around October 31. It marked the end of the harvest season. It marked the beginning of winter. Winter is the darker half of the year.
- Fenrir was held by magical chains. The dwarfs called them Gleipnir. The chains were made from mountain roots, fish's breath, the sound of a cat's footfall, bear's muscles, woman's beard, and bird spit.
- The gates of hell have different names. Helgrind means "hell gate." Nagrind means "corpse gate." Valgrind also means "corpse gate."
- Death from old age or sickness was called "straw death." People would die in their beds. Beds were made of straw back then.
- Vikings were Norse warriors. They thought dying in battle was the best way to die. The worst way to die was from doing crimes. The worst crimes were killing, cheating, and breaking promises.
- Nidhogg was part of the world's balance. He represented evil. He was at the roots of the World Tree. A great eagle represented good. It hung out in the World Tree's top branches. A squirrel ran up and down the tree trunk. It carried messages between the two.
- Norse people had a tradition. They trimmed dead people's hair and nails. They did this before burying them.

CONSIDER THIS!

TAKE A POSITION! Odin kicked Hel out of Asgard. Why did he do this? Do you think Hel was treated badly? Why or why not? Argue your point with reasons and evidence.

SAY WHAT? Reread the 45th Parallel Press book about Freya. Freya was a goddess of death. Hel was the goddess of the dead. Compare them. Explain how they're the same. Explain how they're different.

THINK ABOUT IT! "Hell hath no fury like a woman scorned." This was a famous quote. It comes from a play. The play was called *The Mourning Bride*. It's written by William Congreve. What does this quote mean to you? How does it fit Hel?

LEARN MORE

Dahl, Michael, and Eduardo Garcia (illust.). *Twilight of the Gods—Norse Myths: A Viking Graphic Novel*. North Mankato, MN: Stone Arch Books, 2017.

Ganeri, Anita. *Norse Myths and Legends*. Chicago: Raintree, 2013.

Napoli, Donna Jo, and Christina Balit (illust.). *Treasury of Norse Mythology: Stories of Intrigue, Trickery, Love, and Revenge*. Washington, DC: National Geographic, 2015.

GLOSSARY

Asgard (AHS-gahrd) center of the universe where the Aesir gods lived

corpses (KORPS-iz) dead bodies

giantess (JYE-uhn-tis) female giant

hellhound (HEL-hound) dogs of hell

Norse (NORS) coming from the Norway area

omen (OH-muhn) sign of bad or good things to come

Ragnarok (RAHG-nuh-rok) the final battle of the gods' world, marking the end of their world

serpent (SUR-puhnt) snake

sleet (SLEET) frozen rain

underworld (UHN-dur-wurld) the place where the souls of dead people go after they die

Valhalla (val-HAL-uh) hall of the dead where killed warriors are welcomed

INDEX